CHRISTINA DEMARA

MEANINGFUL
TEACHER

Leadership

REFLECTION, REFINEMENT, AND STUDENT ACHIEVEMENT
INTERACTIVE ACTIVITIES AND JOURNALING

All Rights Reserved

MEANINGFUL TEACHER LEADERSHIP
REFLECTION, REFINEMENT, AND STUDENT ACHIEVEMENT
INTERACTIVE ACTIVITIES & JOURNALING

Published by DeMara-Kirby & Associates, LLC.
P.O. Box 720335 McAllen, Texas 78504
Printed in the United States of America
The United States of America Library of Congress
© 2017 Christina E. DeMara-Kirby

Christina DeMara and her affiliate DeMara-Kirby & Associates, LLC. are committed to planting seeds of knowledge and faith. For public speaking engagements or bulk book orders, please contact us at christinademara.com or EarlyLifeLeadership.com

Also Written By

CHRISTINA DEMARA

My Prayer Book

Peace is Mine
The Forgiveness Journal

I'm Not Broken
*The Power of Prayer, Scripture, and
Interactive Journaling*

How God Saved Me
*My Mother's Memoirs on Abuse,
Depression & Overeating*

The I Am Journal
A Soul-Searching Journal for Creative Women of God

Isaiah 43:2
*40 Days of Scriptures, Reflection, and
Journaling for the Lent Season*

Meaningful

Books & Resources

Meaningful Leadership
How to Build Indestructible Relationships with Your Team Members Through Intentionality and Faith

Meaningful Leadership Journal

Meaningful Leadership Prayer Book

Meaningful Teacher Leadership
Reflection, Refinement, and Student Achievement

Meaningful Writing & Self-Publishing
Your Guide to Igniting Your Pen, Faith, Creativity & Entrepreneurship

Early Life Leadership

Books and Resources

Early Life Leadership in Children
101 Strategies to Grow Great Leaders

Early Life Leadership
101 Conversation Starters and Writing Prompts

Early Life Leadership Workbook
101 Strategies to Grow Great Leaders

Early Life Leadership Workbook for Girls
101 Strategies to Grow Great Leaders

Early Life Leadership Kids Journal

Early Life Leadership in the Classroom
Resources, Strategies & Tidbits to Grow Great Leaders

TABLE OF CONTENTS

Meaningful Teacher Leadership Overview

Our schools are full of hardworking teachers who have accepted the challenging role of "teacher leader." This research-based handbook is a creative way to build, sustain, and expand teacher leaders on any college or school campus. *Meaningful Teacher Leadership: Reflection, Refinement, and Student Achievement* offers a new standard of learning. This book is an interactive journal with twelve sections of activities and thought-provoking questions. Christina DeMara is known for her creative vision and developed this book to ignite thinking, reflection, refinement, and growth, all while engaging in hands-on activities and journaling. *Meaningful Teacher Leadership* is designed to be a resource not only for teacher leaders, but also for college students and administrators who want to support the development of student achievement.

Meaningful Teacher Leadership **is:**

- *Creative, engaging, and thought-provoking.*
- *An organized way to hold yourself or others accountable.*
- *A ready-to-go tool for meetings, classes, or book studies.*

Meaningful Teacher Leadership **entails:**

- *Leadership skill reflections and case studies.*
- *Weekly celebrations.*
- *Meaningful goal-setting.*
- *Teacher leadership self-reflection.*

KNOW: What do I know about Leadership?

FLOW: What is flowing smoothly? What are the things that are going well in the leadership aspect of my life?

GLOW: How do I stand out?

TOW: What am I towing that may be slowing me down from reaching my full leadership potential?

SHOW: What do I show others? How do others perceive me?

BOW & ARROW: What am I ready to launch forward?

GROW: How am I growing as a leader? What am I doing to improve my leadership skills?

LOW: What is an area of weakness I need to work on?

SNOW: What is cold in my leadership life that requires attention?

SOW: What am I working on? Remember, you reap what you sow!

BOWL: What is in my bowl? What leadership resources do I have available to me?

ROW: What am I rowing towards? Am I going in the right direction?

MOW: What is mowing me down and stopping me from moving to the next level of leadership greatness?

OWE: Who do I owe for mentoring me? What am I taking away from my mentors?

Meaningful Teacher Leadership encourages self-reflection, refinement, and student achievement. This book was developed for lead teachers, coaches, strategists, grade-level leaders, department and content leaders, teacher mentors, and for post-secondary teacher programs.

This Book Has 10 Intentions

1. UNDERSTANDING

To provide an understanding of the importance of reflection and how it drives teacher leadership and student success.

2. IGNITE

To ignite self-reflection and self-awareness.

3. LEADERSHIP DIARY

To promote journaling that documents leadership experiences, ideas, growth, and thoughts.

4. REFLECTION

To go back, read, reflect, and comment on what you have previously written. It is always great to look back and see how far you have come.

5. ACCOUNTABILITY

To hold yourself accountable for leadership growth.

6. BOOK STUDY & PROFESSIONAL LEARNING COMMUNITIES

To use as a tool to lead a professional learning community for teacher leadership. This workbook is an excellent way to bond with your teammates while growing together. *Meaningful Teacher Leadership* may be utilized by grade level, content area, or for a campus, district leadership team, or college program.

7. INDEPENDENT PERSONAL GROWTH

To help grow yourself as a teacher leader.

8. ENCOURAGE CHANGE

Through the reflection process, ignite change for organizational structure.

9. PROFESSIONAL / SELF-GROWTH ARTIFACT

This book may be used as an artifact for your teacher evaluation or part of a teacher portfolio.

10. MENTORSHIP TOOL

This is an excellent tool to be used by mentors and mentees.

Dear Meaningful Teacher Leaders,

As I reflect on my first day of teaching, I remember how nervous I was. I remember how much effort I had put into being organized and decorating my classroom. I think I was more nervous than my students were. I quickly learned that my job wasn't just to teach. I was a mom, counselor, nurse, custodian, reading strategist, and a "teacher leader," all in my own right because that's what my students needed from me to be successful. I know you all can relate. I was given a lot of responsibility quickly as a teacher. During my second year of teaching, I worked on a grant for intervention programs for students who had been retained for academic, behavior, and attendance issues, as well as worked with Special Education students while tutoring on the weekends. We can all agree that teachers give a lot of themselves to their career. Unknowingly, I became a teacher leader very quickly. I never experienced any formal training, nor did I have a guide or reflection process to support me along the way. I hope to fill that gap for many of you. I wrote *Meaningful Teacher Leadership* as a tool for all teachers, strategists, mentors, facilitators, department heads, clubs sponsors, grade levels chairs, and for those who just want to strive to be better.

This book was specifically designed to be hands-on, thought-provoking, and personal growth-oriented. The best thing about this book is that there is no right or wrong answer. Your reflections are private, or they can inspire others if you choose to share. The only difficulty for some is honesty, being courageous enough, and being honest about their thoughts, strengths, weakness, and aspirations.

Research shows journaling, drawing, and visual diaries create a more fruitful reflection. I hope this interactive book helps you as much as it has helped me, but most importantly, I hope *Meaningful Teacher Leadership* stimulates your thinking, ignites a craving for growth, and encourages you to grow into the leader you were created to be.

With Warm Wishes and A Heart of Gratitude,

CHRISTINA DEMARA
LIFE • LEARNING • LEADERSHIP

INTRODUCTION

The Rationale for
Meaningful Teacher Leadership:

"I always push myself to do things I am uncomfortable doing or don't know how to do. I think that's how you grow and break personal and professional barriers. If you fail, you learn, and if you are successful, you are on top of the world! But you need to reflect on the processes and path you traveled. Reflection is the key!"
-Christina DeMara

As I have grown in my own leadership abilities, I have realized that a huge component of my personal growth is through reflection and journaling. *Meaningful Teacher Leadership* was designed to encourage the thinking process among leaders at all levels.

The Merriam-Webster Dictionary plainly defines leadership as "the power or ability to lead other people." Leadership has come a long way from assigning tasks from behind a mahogany desk, monitoring profits and execution. Leaders are now teachers, motivators, problem-solvers, team members, creatives, peacemakers, and philanthropists. As we consistently move forward in our leadership growth and development, it is crucial that we are constantly aware of what is going on within us and within our leadership lives. This book was designed to do just that.

What is Meaningful Teacher Leadership Reflection?

DEFINED:

Meaningful Teacher Leadership Reflection is the act of *intentionally* reflecting upon the teaching profession from a leadership perspective in order to achieve success and growth within the classroom and campus.

Meaningful Teacher Leadership was developed to increase student achievement and intentionality while driving student and teacher success. What makes *Meaningful Reflection* different than regular reflection? When reflection is meaningful, it drives, inspires action, and has honest intentions. Without reflection, we cannot lead our students, our clubs, our grade levels, or our content departments to victory. We are not always cognizant of it, but we do reflect all day. It's something that is natural and innate, although, the depth of reflection is not. That's where this book comes in. It is an excellent way to move teachers to the teacher leader level.

Reflection

Refinement

Student Achievement

Meaningful Teacher Leadership Reflection Diagram (DeMara-Kirby, 2017)

What do I need to know about the Meaningful Teacher Leadership activities?

1. There is no right or wrong answer.

2. When you reflect on the activities, turn on your Meaningful Teacher Leader mindset.

3. It is important to know that this book has some recurring activities because it is important to create a baseline of information. At the end of your journey, you can go back and see how far you have come and reflect on how your answers have changed. Your answers will vary depending on what is going on in your life.

4. Reflections are sacred, like prayers. No one can control or stop your reflections. It is okay to keep them private or share whatever you feel comfortable sharing.

5. This book is an excellent way to demonstrate to your principal:

1. You are intentionally working on being successful, so your students can reap the benefits.

2. You are proactive about growing and setting goals.

3. You are a self-motivated, Meaningful Teacher Leader!

Traditional Staff Development

If we reflect on traditional teacher staff development, some sessions usually do not consider the teacher's beliefs, concerns, or interests. Because of this, traditional staff development may not always be successful or satisfying to the educator. Additionally, it does not allow the teacher to reflect because traditional staff development can often be more of a direct teaching session for teachers.

In my research, one of the biggest arguments from educators about traditional staff development is sessions are sometimes chosen or developed by someone outside the classroom. This is likely to result in ownership issues by teachers, which produces a disconnect. In this book, the teacher decides what his or her needs are based on their personal and professional reflections. One teacher may reflect and feel they need technical help, whereas another may conclude they need to work on student engagement. The *Meaningful Teacher Leadership* book creates accountability, ownership, and autonomy.

Through the reflection process, teachers can choose the content, training, mentorship, and development they need to be Meaningful Teacher Leaders inside and outside of the classroom. One of the most powerful things I found in my research was how powerful listening is. When principals listen to their teacher leaders, this helps the principal understand what they need, makes the teacher feel valued, and inspires teacher leaders to make the changes necessary to refine their teaching and teacher leadership abilities (Walker, 1997).

Why is *Meaningful Teacher Leadership* important?

I found the beginning stage of reflection noted as Pre-reflection. Pre-reflection is often reactive and is ignited by a problematic situation, emotional problems, or worry. Through reflection, our minds start racing and coming up with suggestions of what to do and how to fix our problems. If there is more than one option, reflection analysis continues. Reflection not only meets the needs of a solution to a problem, but it may also help ease the uneasiness and emotional constraints. Pre-reflection supports initiate ideas and thoughts, proposed solutions, and connects other reflections through a reasoning process (Boody, 1992).

Reflection is based on the self and significant perceptions that have left an impact on you. They operate in conjunction with shaping the understandings and experiences of the teacher, and their meanings relative to their experience (Pedro, 2001).

Self-correction through reflection is a big piece of the puzzle that is often taken for granted. It is imperative that teacher leaders study and reflect on teaching experiences. Evaluating student achievement and learning skills during a lesson is something that is done and is often seen when we group and regroup our students. It also happens when we put professionals into groups. We listen and think about what the other person is saying, and how it connects to our lives. In Technical Reflection, the teacher reflects on specific tasks. For example, the pronunciation of a letter sound or fine motor skill activities. However, in Descriptive Reflection, a teacher considers the reasons that it would be desirable for a student to acquire a particular learning skill. To recap, in Technical Reflection, we are reflecting on something specific and pinpointed, and with Descriptive Reflection, we are reflecting on the "why" (Gardner, 2011).

Based on my research, I define Teacher Leadership as a teacher who leads and drives student and campus achievement through leading and taking the initiative via self-development activities. Even though there are formal teacher leadership roles, numerous schools have established programs or develop teacher leadership positions and teacher formal leadership roles, such as a master teacher, department chair, team leader, lead teacher, teacher mentor, curriculum specialist, interventionist, and instructional coach. These teacher leadership designations recognize the crucial role of teachers as key players in the extensive effort to improve student achievement. Teacher Leaders also support the overwhelming administrative responsibilities of running an efficient campus. Principals develop and hire strong teacher leaders as partners in order to increase school improvement (www.ocmboces.org, 2017).

Some reflection may include, "What is the reality of the situation? Is my reality the same as the reality of others? Do I understand the problem? Do I have the knowledge to understand the problem? Do I understand the theory? Do I understand how to apply theory?" Teacher leaders who reflect, expose themselves to examining multiple viewpoints from other perspectives in which they examine "contradictions, doubts, dilemmas, and possibilities" (Milligan, 2014).

One of the biggest dilemmas principals face around the world is balance. Principals must view circumstances with the eyes of both management and leadership because they both overlap. Reflection plays a big part in this practice. There is the potential use of mentoring and developing strong teacher leaders (Thompson, 1998). So, it's appropriate to ask "How do we monitor teachers while giving them respect, autonomy, and leadership responsibilities?" That is a tough task. That is where reflection supports all three.

As teachers, we have all reflected on some part of our teaching day. Whether it is on the drive home from work: "Was that the best way to handle that discipline problem with Joey?" Or maybe at the end of a section of an instructional unit, "What can I do differently to make this lesson come alive for my students?" We have all reflected on our teaching and classroom activity. However, for reflection to enhance success and achievement in the classroom, there has to be some structure for reflection, and it should be performed on a regular basis (Stemme, 2005).

Reflective Thinking refers to the process of making knowledgeable and logical judgments on educational matters, then assessing the consequences of those decisions. Teacher leaders should possess knowledge as well as process, analyze, and make the suggestions required to facilitate the best solution to the problem through reflective thinking as a teacher leadership norm (Richardson, 1992).

There are different kinds of reflection. Descriptive Reflection is most likely the easiest reflection for most. This can be done through writing as it is a simple retelling of the event and only requires teacher leaders to report what happened and why. On the downside, it may be the least thought provoking reflection for some as it does not demand the same depth of analysis. Descriptive Reflection is at the lower end of analyzation and requires basic knowledge and recall. Dialogic and Critical Reflection may take more mental energy and time commitment.

Studies have shown that teachers who have participated in written reflection and trends across different aspects of their lives may increase the chances of having a better relationship with dialogic or critical reflection. Reflective writing such as detailed writing, descriptive reflection, Dialogic Reflection, and Critical Reflection used simultaneously have been to strengthen engagement in written reflection within all three categories (descriptive reflection, dialogic reflection, and critical reflection) (Wilson, 2013).

Teachers have stated that, by reflecting, they felt...

1. More empowered to formulate solutions to obstacles they faced personally or at work.

2. Visionary, because they clearly thought through obstacles from a diversity of viewpoints before deciding on an action.

3. Intelligent and more creative because they

practiced their negotiating and influencing skills to convince others to reflect and enact change, which resulted in increased self-esteem related to job experience and execution.

4. Better knowing they received mental exercise while increasing their intellectual awareness. When teacher leaders became intellectually aware of their inner reflective states, they appeared to become cognizant of creative ideas, and able to provide solutions through critical thinking via a wide variety of problems they faced in work or home environments (Milligan, 2014).

Content Reflection is the level where teacher leaders examine the content of an issue or problem by reflecting on perceptions and asking "what" questions. Eventually, through reflective practices, they are led to process reflection, where they begin to ask "how" questions and use problem-solving techniques to examine an issue or perception and then look at how effectively it can be carried through. Teachers need to ask "why" questions and see what change is needed from within, so a transformation can take place. Critical reflection occurs when the underlying beliefs or ideas are questioned (Mezirow, 1991).

The idea of reflection as a way to improve teacher practice and also prepare teachers for the classroom is usually centered on written reflections (Campoy, 2000). Written reflections, as a part of written assignments, often take the form of teacher candidates looking at what happened during the week, analyzing how they reacted during the situation, and evaluating how they would better handle the situation in the future. In some cases, there may be even more limited opportunities for teachers to move beyond the limited written reflections on content because face-to-face interaction is sometimes impossible. Thus, the written reflective assignments do not go far enough to accomplish the real goals of reflection, which are guiding teachers from a self-concerned approach of teaching and being focused on class control to a more automated approach that helps them adapt lessons to meet the needs of students (Calderhead & Robson, 1991). Teachers, particularly new teachers, have trouble blending their practical experiences with their previous learning, as well as with educational practices and theories they study in their teacher preparation courses. There are three likely reasons or some combination of these reasons that teacher goals are not accomplished as often as expected. These reasons are the disconnection of the content of instruction, lack of scaffolded practices, and negative previous experience (Love, 2009).

Meaningful Teacher Leaders must be provided with opportunities to reflect upon and refine their emotional responses to situations that call for leadership. Reflection and feedback on behavior and emotions are the critical components of learning. Cognitive understanding is the center of leadership development (D'Cruz, 2003). When teachers connect to a deeper reflective state for correction at the level of descriptive reflection, they are doing more than just reporting on their lessons and classroom activity; they are connecting what they did with why, and what they should do differently. At this reflective level, the teacher thinks about and evaluates his decisions and actions during class. A teacher might do this within classes, during a lunch break, during a preparation period, on the drive home, or whenever the teacher leader has time to reflect on a particular classroom experience (Gardner, 2011).

Meaningful Teacher Leadership was developed to support teachers, so they can have a high impact on student achievement and success while conserving time and energy. Many times, the teacher is taking work home, making copies, and cutting paper for foldables ahead of time in hopes of creating a high impact on student learning. But if you stop to reflect and look at things with the precision of hitting a target with a bow and arrow, you can make a bigger impact through meaningful reflection.

Why is Meaningful Teacher Leadership Reflection Important?

Reflection is part of personal growth, self-awareness, and goal achievements. Without reflection, we become stagnant.

"IF I STRIVE TO BE THE BEST I CAN BE, MY STUDENTS WILL BENEFIT."

As you move forward in the book, there are four components that will have an affect on your thoughts and written reflections.

4 COMPONENTS THAT AFFECT OUR REFLECTIONS

1. Teaching Experience & Beliefs
2. Professional Experience & Beliefs
3. Personal Experience & Beliefs
4. Spirituality / Community Life Experiences & Beliefs

Defining Teacher Refinement:

Teacher Refinement is an intentional behavior by a teacher to increase achievement and success.

*Reminder: Through Meaningful Refinement, we are refining and adjusting ourselves first. Through those adjustments, student success and achievements may follow.

Five examples of proactive Meaningful Teacher Leadership Reflections and Refinement in the classroom:

1. Refining a lesson: Reteaching using different activities, interests of students, and/or learning styles versus blaming the student.

Why? Teacher Leaders reflect on their actions when they are not successful. Some questions they might ask are, "What can I do differently? Why didn't that lesson come out like planned?"

2. Refining classroom behavior: Setting up a cell phone charging station to limit cell phone usage versus getting upset and frustrated during instruction.

Why? Teacher Leaders are very cognizant of where they spend their energy, and they also know how quickly things can turn into a power struggle. They understand that being proactive saves time, energy, and frustration.

Some questions they ask are, "How can I make my classroom run smoother? How can I build a strong professional relationship with my students? Is there a mutual respect in my classroom?"

3. Refining professional relationships: Spending professional time learning from the campus administration and other teachers versus isolating oneself.

Why? Teacher Leaders value people, learning, and understand there is always something new to learn. Some questions they ask are, "What can I learn from the other professionals I work with? What do others know and do that may help my students be more successful?"

4. Refining grade level or content area relationships: Practice an open door/open dialogue relationship with your teammates versus an "I work better alone" mentality.

Why? Teacher Leaders know how valuable the relationships with their teammates are. Some questions they ask are, "What are they doing with their students that works for them?" "What can I contribute to my teammates?"

5. Refining your relationship with the community: Invite community members, business owners, and community leaders to talk to your students versus teacher-centered presentations.

Why? Teacher Leaders think outside the box and understand the importance of community and real-life connections. Some questions they ask are, "How can the community make a positive impact on my students and their learning? How can I change things up in my classroom?"

Refinement is a crucial component of student success and achievement, your annual teacher evaluation, and for your professional growth. The state of Texas has included refinement in their 2017 educator's evaluation system called Texas Teacher Evaluation and Support System (www.teachfortexas.org). After reflecting and understanding yourself on a deeper level (self-awareness), it's time to take action! We can't change things overnight, but we can set small achievable goals through small reflective steps.

SECTION

1

"Understanding"

The Meaningful Teacher Leadership Reflection Definitions

MENTAL IMPRINT ICON	DEFINING REFLECTION ICONS
	KNOW: What do I know about leadership?
	GLOW: How do I stand out?
	SHOW: What do I show others? How do others perceive me?
	GROW: How am I growing as a leader? What am I doing to improve my leadership skills?
	SNOW: What is cold in my leadership life that requires attention?
	BOWL: What is in my bowl? What leadership resources do I have available to me?
	MOW: What is mowing me down and stopping me from moving to the next level of leadership greatness?

MENTAL IMPRINT ICON	DEFINING REFLECTION ICONS
	FLOW: What is flowing smoothly? What are the things that are going well in the leadership aspect of my life?
	TOW: What am I towing that may be slowing me down from reaching my full leadership potential?
	BOW & ARROW: What am I ready to launch forward?
	LOW: What is an area of weakness I need to work on?
	SOW: What am I working on? Remember, you reap what you sow!
	ROW: What am I rowing towards? Am I going in the right direction?
	OWE: Who do I owe for mentoring me? What am I taking away from my mentors?

"KNOW"

What do I know about leadership?

We all know different things about leadership. All the experiences we've had since childhood have molded us into the leaders we are today, whether we realize it or not. We have been sculpted by abrasive coaches, nurturing grandmothers, and our school teachers. The illustration on the next page describes the modeling leadership journey. Starting in the middle, the smallest targeted area resembles the leadership planted in us throughout our childhood based on our experiences in school and with family and trusted adults. The second targeted area is titled "Primary Work Experience."

Leadership concepts are acquired through our first jobs and community experiences as young adults. The third targeted area is titled "Formal Schooling." It does not matter what your degree is in, all educational sectors teach some component of leadership, ethics, and management. The fourth targeted area is "Professional Work Experience." This is where professionals continue to build on the other areas through experiences in a leadership or management role. The fifth and final targeted area is "Personal Growth." This is the act of self-educating through mentors, books, and podcasts.

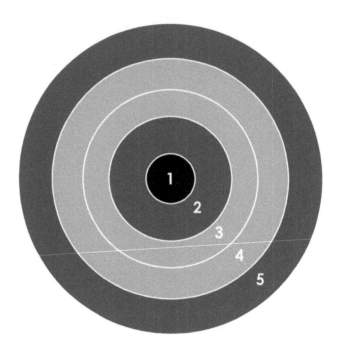

1. Childhood Experiences & Family

2. Primary Work Experience

3. Formal Schooling

4. Professional Work Experience

5. Personal Growth

My Primary Leadership Reflection

⛨ Childhood Experiences & Family

_____

_____

_____

_____

⛨ Primary Work Experience

_____

_____

_____

_____

⊕ Formal Schooling

_____

_____

_____

_____

⊕ Professional Work Experience

_____

_____

_____

_____

⊕ Personal Growth

_____

_____

_____

_____

Meaningful Refection Processes

Level 1: Understanding

There are three components of the levels illustrated below. Pros, Cons, and Visualize are at level one because they require minimal levels of thinking and planning.

MEANINGFUL REFLECTION QUESTIONS		
PROS What is the good that will come out of this?	CONS What is the bad that will come out of this?	VISUALIZE What does goal completion look like?

Level 2: Analysis

The analysis includes measurement, an action that needs to be taken, and a plan of action for successful execution.

MEANINGFUL REFLECTION QUESTIONS *COLLECT DATA AND ARTIFACTS.		
MEASUREMENT How will I measure my progress?	VERBS What action needs to be taken?	WHY? Always ask why and why again.

"GLOW"

WHAT ARE MY STRENGTHS?

The "glow" icon was designed to provoke the thinking and refection of your strengths. What are the characteristics that make you glow and stand out? Knowing your strengths can be difficult and knowing when to use them can be even harder. In leadership, it is inferred that we have the ability to lead and guide followers toward a vision or goal. We possess many strengths. Please see the characteristic bank and reflect on your strengths. Ultimately, our strengths are situational and should be used as needed.

Think about the traits on the grid on the next page and put a star next to the traits that you think you possess. Then call three people. Write one (first call) next to the three traits the first caller uses to describe you as a leader. Call the second person and place a two next to the three traits they say you possess, and so on. I recommend that you try to call people from different aspects of your life.

Persever-ance	"Critical Thinker"	Well-rounded	Private	Open-minded
"Good Listener"	Focused	Optimistic	Street-smart	Resourceful
Commu-nicator	Lover of Learning	Innovative	Ethical	Diligent
Creative	Respectful	Original	Open to Change	Trustworthy
Conservative	Kind	"Naturally Curious"	Ingenuity	Brave
"Emotionally Stable "	Productive	Insightful	Social	"Emotionally Intelligent "
Honest	Forgiving	Fair	Spiritual	Peace-maker
Authentic	Self-con-trolled	Humorous	Self-aware	Takes Charge
Enthusiastic	Loyal	Generous	Motivational	Discreet
Intuitive	Compassion	Patient	Charismatic	Collab-orative
Writer	Mathe-matician	Historian	Mechanical	Artistic
Reader	Forgiving	"The Mentor"	"The Minimalist "	Tech-savvy

"SHOW"

WHAT DO I SHOW OTHERS?
HOW DO OTHERS PERCEIVE ME?

There are many reasons why people stand out. Some leaders stand out because they are yellers, and some stand out because they have been seen helping the custodial staff because something needs to get done. The only way one can truly answer these questions honestly is by being self-aware. Self-awareness is the act of truly understanding who you are: the good, bad, and the ugly.

For example, if you ask me what one of my strengths are, I would say that I am focused and consistent. My husband doesn't always see that in me. At times, he sees that I can be absorbed and inattentive because I am working on other things. It is all about perception.

What do I show others?

_____

_____

_____

How do others perceive me?

_____

_____

_____

What do I need to adjust and work on?

_____

_____

_____

"GROW"

HOW AM I GROWING AS A LEADER?
WHAT AM I DOING TO IMPROVE MY LEADERSHIP SKILLS?

WHAT LEADERSHIP SKILL DO I NEED TO IMPROVE?	WHAT IS MY GROWTH STRATEGY OR TOOL?	WHAT IS MY GOAL?	WHEN IS MY FINISH DATE?	WHAT OUTCOME AM I AIMING FOR?

What am I planting in my teacher leadership life to help myself grow?

_____

_____

_____

How am I nurturing my leadership skills?

_____

_____

_____

What do I want to harvest in my leadership life?

_____

_____

_____

"SNOW"

What is cold in my leadership life and requires immediate attention?

Our bodies are conditioned to keep our core warm, our core that contains our heart and major organs. At times, that is how we treat the things going on in our lives. We only address and give attention to the major things. We leave some things cold, like working out, personal reading, and time with our loved ones. It is essential that we understand why these tasks have been left cold. Is leaving aspects of your life cold a bad thing? No. Sometimes, we need to stop juggling and give intentional attention to the people or projects in front of us in that moment. For example, our health or the health of someone we love. Our personal relationships and families also need intentional time. Therefore, we need to leave marathon training or volunteering cold. There are other things that need immediate attention.

On the other end of the spectrum, some of us have left crucial tasks unattended, such as goals we have set for our team or organization, our health, and our personal growth. Falling into survival mode, some have the mentality of, "I will move when the fire comes." This type of attitude is also dangerous. I know it's hard to keep all aspects of your life flourishing, but it's essential to reflect on your life as a teacher leader. What has grown cold in your leadership life and requires immediate attention?

WHAT AM I DOING WITH MY EXTRA TIME THAT MAY BE LEAVING OTHER TASKS OR PEOPLE IN MY LIFE COLD?	WHAT ARE SOME THINGS I CAN REMOVE FROM MY LIFE?
☐	☐
☐	☐
☐	☐
☐	☐
☐	☐
WHAT AREAS IN MY FAMILY LIFE ARE COLD?	WHAT AREAS IN MY COMMUNITY LIFE OR PERSONAL FRIENDSHIPS ARE COLD?
☐	☐
☐	☐
☐	☐
☐	☐
☐	☐

	❄️ WHAT IS COMPLETELY COLD IN MY LIFE?	🌧️ WHAT AM I CURRENTLY STRUGGLING WITH?	☀️ WHERE AM I INVESTING MOST OF MY TIME?
💡 Ideas			
❤️ Family & Friends			
🎯 Goals			
🤝 Relationships			

"BOW + ARROW"

What am I ready to launch forward?

When you think about a bow and arrow and the art of archery, this sport is one that is focused and precise. To hit your target, you must pull the arrow back, aim with a hawk eye, hold with a steady hand, and release with intensity. It is the same thing for your leadership life. The career carousel is moving faster and faster thanks to technology. Oftentimes, part of the reflection process is stopping and holding back, just like we do with the arrow. One of the biggest misconceptions in leadership is, "Once I make a decision, I can't take it back." Nothing could be further from the truth. In leadership, you must be able to say, "Stop! This isn't working. We need to put everything on hold in order to launch this onward with the utmost integrity." This icon was intended to ignite questions such as, "Where am I going? What does moving forward look like? What do I need to spend more time on in order to move forward? Just like the arrow is being pulled back, in order to hit its target, we also have to take a few steps back in order to move forward in the right direction.

Reflect on what you are holding back and launching forward in your life. You may concentrate on your professional life only or reflect on your life overall. Many times, things overlap in your professional and personal life. Continuing to the second column, give three reasons why you are launching forward or holding back.

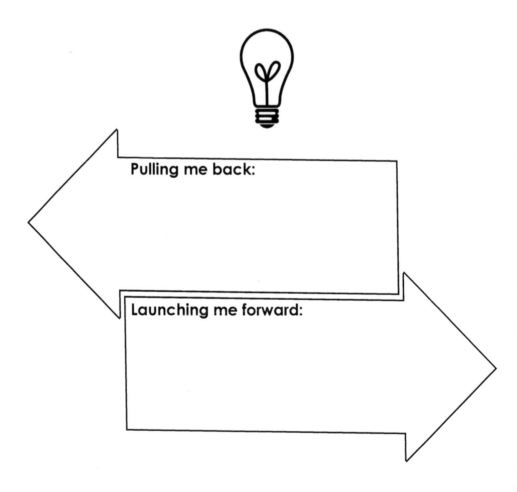

Pulling me back:

Launching me forward:

"FLOW"

WHAT IS FLOWING IN MY LIFE?

What is "flow"? Flow is something in your life that is going smoothly. That does not mean that everything is great and flourishing. It just means that there are bigger fish to fry. This "flow" does not need immediate attention and represents contentment. For example, at Store A, the manager and his team members are doing okay. There are no big issues. On the outside, the store is running and serving customers efficiently. There is no growth or immediate fire. Whereas, at Store B, the manager and team members are having trouble getting along, and if it is not one thing, it is another. Customers are often leaving unsatisfied. There is no "flow," and things are not running smoothly.

When I reflected on my life, I found that in my professional life, I was content with my staff and my personal development. Why? I had good professional relationships with my team, but I wasn't digging deeper. I wasn't being intentional about getting to know them or their gifts. Secondly, my personal development was flowing because I was in graduate school, so I felt I was in class and learning. I was doing fine. But the truth was, I wasn't learning holistically. Instead, I was concentrating on the specific constructs of those classes.

Below, think about your life. What is flowing in your life? These might be things you take for granted. In the second column, think about why. Then, in the last column, reflect and how you can adjust to change.

What is flowing in my life?	Why?	How can I increase or decrease the flow?

"TOW"

WHAT ARE THE PERSONAL AND PROFESSIONAL BURDENS I AM TOWING AND CARRYING AROUND?

When your car breaks down, you need to call a tow truck to take it to the mechanic. Now think of this in terms of leadership and think of yourself as a leader. You are the tow truck that takes and guides the heavy car to the mechanic. Think about what you may be towing that is preventing you from reaching your full leadership potential. What are the things in your life that are broken or need replacement? When we get our vehicles towed, sometimes we must choose to fix the car and sometimes we must cut our losses.

What are the personal and professional burdens you are towing and carrying around?

- *Professional Tow*

- *Personal Tow*

- *Professional Tow*

- *Personal Tow*

- *Professional Tow*

"LOW"

WHAT IS AN AREA OF WEAKNESS I NEED TO WORK ON?

Oftentimes, this answer is easy, sometimes it's not, and sometimes we have a false perception of our weakness. What we see every so often is not what others see. I always profess an open-door policy. I invite my teammates to disagree with me, share ideas on how to make things better, and I invite open constructive criticism. One thing I have been told is, "What comes out of my mouth sometimes doesn't match what I expected." This puts me and my teammates on different pages and wastes time and energy. I know what I want, but the words from my brain to my mouth are not being executed effectively. I know what I mean, but others need to know also. I fixed this weakness by using handwritten drawings, visuals, and examples. This helps make things more cohesive.

I challenge you to call three personal friends and relatives and ask them for three of your weaknesses. Challenge yourself even further and ask three vertical (upper, middle, and lower management) staff members what your weaknesses are. Do not take things personally. Ask for examples and reflect. This is great data to have in order to make yourself better.

WHAT IS AN AREA OF WEAKNESS I NEED TO WORK ON?

I Called...
Notes

I Called...
Notes

I Called…
Notes

I Called…
Notes

I Called…
Notes

I Called…
Notes

"SOW"

WHAT AM I WORKING ON?
WHAT SEEDS AM I PLANTING FOR A BETTER TOMORROW?

When you plant seeds in the soil, you sow them. You can also sow things like ideas. If your ideas (or your seeds) develop and grow, you've successfully sown them. Think about your life. "What am I working on?" Remember, you reap what you sow!

What seeds am I planting?

_____

_____

_____

How do I nurture the seeds?

_____

_____

_____

What do I want to harvest?

_____

_____

_____

"ROW"

WHAT AM I ROWING TOWARDS?
WHAT AM I WORKING ON?

When you look at someone rowing a boat, it looks like they are only using their upper body, but many athletes will tell you the rowing strokes come from their legs. Just like in life, sometimes people are perceived to have it easy or "be lucky," but no one knows the hard work and late hours you have put into your craft. There is more than meets the eye in rowing and in life.

REFLECTION QUESTIONS

What am I rowing towards?

_____

_____

Am I going in the right direction?

_____

_____

Am I being intentional?

_____

_____

"OWE"

Who do I owe for mentoring and guiding me? Who are the leaders in my life who have made me better? What advice or life lessons am I taking away from my mentors?

Think about where you are today. There have been family, friends, professors, and mentors that have gotten you to this point in your career and life. Personally, my mom helped babysit my children while I was in college. She gave me peace of mind knowing my children were safe and well taken care of. There were also principals and local community leaders who mentored and believed in me. There were many skills I learned from them. Do you remember the big target on page 42? Reflect on all the leaders who have made you better, and look forward to all the students you will make better.

WHO DO I OWE FOR MENTORING ME?	PROFESSIONAL ADVICE LIFE LESSONS RECOMMENDATIONS	SEND A "THANK YOU" CARD!
		☐
		☐
		☐
		☐

"MOW"

WHAT IS MOWING ME DOWN AND STOPPING ME FROM MOVING TO THE NEXT LEVEL OF LEADERSHIP GREATNESS?

Throughout our lives, there are circumstances or people who are mowing us down. This often looks like spiteful people at work, a family illness, or anything negative that is stopping us from reaching our full potential. Like the lawn mower, when the grass is cut too short, it will burn and break down. If we don't reflect on these things, we will mentally and emotionally burn out.

What are some things I need to cut out of my life?

Things cut you short and stop you from accomplishing tasks or goals.

What is cutting me short or taking up my time?

_____

_____

Things that mow you down often leave you tired and drained.

What is mowing me down?

_____

_____

What is stopping me from moving to the next level of leadership greatness?

_____

_____

"BOWL"

Whаt is in my bowl?

What leadership resources do I have available to me?

As teachers, we love our schedules and routines. It is very easy to stick to our routines. After all, it is our routines that help us get everything done, and keep our students on track. The only drawback of routines is that they keep us in one place, leaving us no time to learn and implement new resources.

What is in your bowl?

What are three tools you use every day?

1. _____

2. _____

3. _____

What resources do you have available that you are not using and why?

_____

_____

_____

As a teacher leader, how can you diversify the tools you use on campus?

_____

_____

_____

Some ideas may include:

- *Resource of the Week*
- *Teacher Tools Monthly*
- *Five-Minute Presentations during staff meetings*
- *Networking with other campuses to get feedback on teacher tools*

Gather Data and Make a Consensus

Ask three other teachers: "What are three teacher tools you can't live without?"

Teacher 1

1. _____

2. _____

3. _____

Teacher 2

1. _____

2. _____

3. _____

Teacher 3

1. _____

2. _____

3. _____

SECTION 2

INTENTIONALITY

INTENTIONALITY IS WHEN WE STOP, ENGAGE, AND GIVE
SPECIAL ATTENTION TO SOMETHING OR SOMEONE

Q1. Why is intentionality an important leadership skill?	Q2. What does intentionally have to do with different personalities and work ethics?	Q3. As a leader, what are some things that you must always be intentional about?
Answer:	Answer:	Answer:
Why? (Defend Your Answer)	Why? (Defend Your Answer)	Why? (Defend Your Answer)

WHAT ARE SOME OBSTACLES PREVENTING
YOU FROM BEING INTENTIONAL?

Case Study 1

Emma Garcia is a first-year teacher. She is young and tech-savvy. She holds a bachelor's degree in elementary education and a master's degree in English. After the first week of back-to-school meetings and training, several campus staff members noticed she was distracted and disconnected. Her classroom is Pinterest-worthy, and she has not voiced any issues. Reflect and answer the questions below.

Meaningful Teacher Leadership Reflection

Q1. Ms. Garcia appears disengaged from her team members. How can you as a Meaningful Teacher Leader change that?

_____

_____

_____

_____

_____

Q2. As a Meaningful Teacher Leader, what strengths and weakness do you see in Ms. Garcia? How can you utilize her strengths and help her with her weaknesses?

_____

_____

_____

_____

_____

Q3. How can you build a relationship with someone who isn't ready or who has maybe had previous negative experiences?

_____

_____

_____

_____

_____

Case Study 2

- *Every year for the last four years, Johnston Middle School has outperformed all other middle schools across the region, especially in writing and science.*

- *Every year, Johnston Middle School has a new principal.*

- *Every year, Johnston Middle School has large groups of students who are mobile due to migrant field work, pipeline jobs, and the local oil refinery hiring and firing employees.*

A. What are 3 things you can infer about Johnston Middle School?

1. _____

2. _____

3. _____

B. How is Johnston outperforming everyone? What can you infer are their 3 strengths?

1. _____

2. _____

3. _____

C. What are some things Johnston Middle School teachers can do to be prepared for the kids who are coming and going all year?

1. _____

2. _____

3. _____

_____

MEANINGFUL GOALS

HEALTH

□
□
□
□
□
□
□
□

HEART & SPIRITUALITY

□
□
□
□
□
□
□
□

FAMILY

□
□
□
□
□
□
□
□

COMMUNITY & FRIENDS

□
□
□
□
□
□
□
□

PROBLEM SOLVING & PERSEVERING THROUGH OBSTACLES

OBSTACLE	PLAN A	PLAN B	OUTCOME

OBSTACLE	PLAN A	PLAN B	OUTCOME

MEANINGFUL TEACHER LEADERSHIP CELEBRATIONS

1	
2	
3	
4	
5	
6	
7	

SECTION
3

LEADERSHIP SKILL HIGHLIGHT
LISTENING

LISTENING IS WHEN WE MAKE A CONSCIENTIOUS EFFORT TO
HEAR AND UNDERSTAND WHAT IS BEING COMMUNICATED.

Q1. Why is listening an important leadership skill?	Q2. What does listening create? Or change?	Q3. As a leader, what are some things you can do to be a good listener to both your team members and students?
Answer:	Answer:	Answer:
Why? (Defend Your Answer)	Why? (Defend Your Answer)	Why? (Defend Your Answer)

WHAT ARE SOME OBSTACLES PREVENTING
YOU FROM BEING A GOOD LISTENER?

Memorization Icon	"OW" Leadership Reflection	Internalization What does that look like? Draw a picture or symbol.	What do I need to do to nurture this area?
	KNOW: What do I know about leadership?		
	GLOW: What are my leadership qualities that glow? How do I stand out?		
	SHOW: What do I show others? How do others perceive me?		
	GROW: How am I growing as a leader? What am I doing to improve my leadership skills?		
	SNOW: What is cold in my leadership life that requires attention?		
	BOWL: What is in my bowl? What leadership resources do I have?		
	MOW: What is mowing me down and stopping me from moving to the next level of leadership greatness?		

Memorization Icon	"OW" Leadership Reflection	Internalization What does that look like? Draw a picture or symbol.	What do I need to do to nurture this area?
	FLOW: What is flowing smoothly? What are the things going good in the leadership aspect of my life?		
	TOW: What am I towing that may be slowing me down from reaching my full leadership potential?		
	BOW: What am I ready to launch forward?		
	LOW: What is an area of weakness I need to work on?		
	SOW: What am I working on? Remember, you reap what you sow!		
	ROW: What am I rowing towards? Am I going in the right direction?		
	OWE: Who do I owe for mentoring me? What am I taking away from my mentors?		

Meaningful Teacher Reflection

Listening looks like

_____

Listening helps

_____

Listening provides

_____

Listening increases

_____

Listening will

_____

MEANINGFUL GOALS

HEALTH

- [ ]
- [ ]
- [ ]
- [ ]
- [ ]
- [ ]
- [ ]
- [ ]

HEART & SPIRITUALITY

- [ ]
- [ ]
- [ ]
- [ ]
- [ ]
- [ ]
- [ ]
- [ ]

FAMILY

- [ ]
- [ ]
- [ ]
- [ ]
- [ ]
- [ ]
- [ ]
- [ ]

COMMUNITY & FRIENDS

- [ ]
- [ ]
- [ ]
- [ ]
- [ ]
- [ ]
- [ ]
- [ ]

	MEANINGFUL TEACHER LEADERSHIP CELEBRATIONS
1	
2	
3	
4	
5	
6	
7	

SECTION 4

SELF-AWARENESS

SELF-AWARENESS IS HAVING AN HONEST UNDERSTANDING
OF WHO YOU ARE, INCLUDING STRENGTHS,
WEAKNESSES, BELIEFS, AND MOTIVATION.

Q1. Why is self-awareness an important leadership skill?	Q2. What does self-awareness have to do with different personalities and work ethics?	Q3. As a leader, what are some things that you must do in order to have self-awareness?
Answer:	Answer:	Answer:
Why? (Defend Your Answer)	Why? (Defend Your Answer)	Why? (Defend Your Answer)

WHAT ARE SOME OBSTACLES THAT PREVENT YOU FROM HAVING
AN HONEST PERCEPTION (SELF-AWARENESS) OF WHO YOU ARE?

Case Study 1

Mr. Hasberg has been an educator for 30 years. He is currently the Head Junior High School Athletic Coach and a Special Education Teacher. You have noticed that he has been out more frequently on official school business and you are worried that the Special Education students in your grade level are not getting the best of him. You both are cordial, but don't have a strong professional relationship.

Meaningful Teacher Leadership Reflection

Q1. As the 8th Grade Team Leader, how do you address Mr. Hasberg without offending him? What leadership skills do you need to utilize?

_____

_____

_____

_____

_____

Q2. As a Meaningful Teacher Leader, you must have a box of tools. What are some tools you can use to make this situation better for everyone? How can you both walk away from this with a win-win situation?

_____

_____

_____

_____

_____

Case Study 2

As a teacher leader, we are often teamed up with new or inexperienced teachers to mentor. Reflect back to your first year of teaching, who lead you?

Meaningful Teacher Leadership Reflection

Q1. What would you give your mentee that you did not receive?

_____

_____

_____

Q2. What is the most essential leadership skill your mentee needs to learn?

_____

_____

_____

Q3. Why are mentors considered as teacher leaders?

_____

_____

_____

MEANINGFUL TEACHER LEADERSHIP CELEBRATIONS

1	
2	
3	
4	
5	
6	
7	

Problem Solving & Persevering Through Obstacles

Obstacle	Plan A	Plan B	Outcome

Obstacle	Plan A	Plan B	Outcome

What Drives Me

What are some things that motivate you and keep you moving forward?

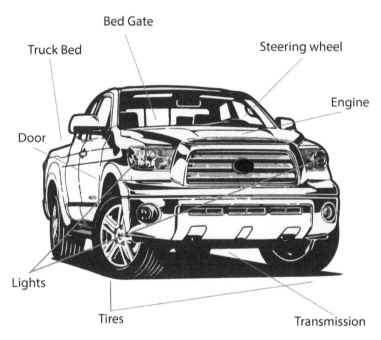

1.	2.	3.	4.
5.	6.	7.	8.

SECTION
5

FORGIVENESS

FORGIVENESS HELPS US LET GO OF YESTERDAY'S GRUDGES AND ANGER. WHEN WE EMBRACE FORGIVENESS, IT ALLOWS US TO MOVE FORWARD AND INTENTIONALLY FOCUS ON WHAT IS IMPORTANT.

Q1. Why is forgiveness an important leadership skill?	Q2. What does forgiveness have to do with different personalities and work ethics?	Q3. As a leader, what are some things that you must do in order to forgive others?
Answer:	Answer:	Answer:
Why? (Defend Your Answer)	Why? (Defend Your Answer)	Why? (Defend Your Answer)

WHAT ARE SOME OBSTACLES THAT PREVENT YOU FROM FORGIVING OTHERS?

MEMORIZATION ICON	"OW" LEADERSHIP REFLECTION	INTERNALIZATION WHAT DOES THAT LOOK LIKE? DRAW A PICTURE OR SYMBOL.	WHAT DO I NEED TO DO TO NURTURE THIS AREA?
	KNOW: What do I know about leadership?		
	GLOW: What are my leadership qualities that glow? How do I stand out?		
	SHOW: What do I show others? How do others perceive me?		
	GROW: How am I growing as a leader? What am I doing to improve my leadership skills?		
	SNOW: What is cold in my leadership life that requires attention?		
	BOWL: What is in my bowl? What leadership resources do I have?		
	MOW: What is mowing me down and stopping me from moving to the next level of leadership greatness?		

MEMORIZATION ICON	"OW" LEADERSHIP REFLECTION	INTERNALIZATION WHAT DOES THAT LOOK LIKE? DRAW A PICTURE OR SYMBOL.	WHAT DO I NEED TO DO TO NURTURE THIS AREA?
	FLOW: What is flowing smoothly? What are the things going good in the leadership aspect of my life?		
	TOW: What am I towing that may be slowing me down from reaching my full leadership potential?		
	BOW: What am I ready to launch forward?		
	LOW: What is an area of weakness I need to work on?		
	SOW: What am I working on? Remember, you reap what you sow!		
	ROW: What am I rowing towards? Am I going in the right direction?		
	OWE: Who do I owe for mentoring me? What am I taking away from my mentors?		

MEANINGFUL GOALS

HEALTH

- [ ]
- [ ]
- [ ]
- [ ]
- [ ]
- [ ]
- [ ]
- [ ]

HEART & SPIRITUALITY

- [ ]
- [ ]
- [ ]
- [ ]
- [ ]
- [ ]
- [ ]
- [ ]

FAMILY

- [ ]
- [ ]
- [ ]
- [ ]
- [ ]
- [ ]
- [ ]
- [ ]

COMMUNITY & FRIENDS

- [ ]
- [ ]
- [ ]
- [ ]
- [ ]
- [ ]
- [ ]
- [ ]

MEANINGFUL TEACHER LEADERSHIP CELEBRATIONS

1	
2	
3	
4	
5	
6	
7	

What is thriving and growing in your leadership life?

SECTION

6

POSITIVE PERCEPTION

A POSITIVE PERCEPTION IS ESSENTIAL TO HAVING A SUCCESSFUL DAY. WHEN WE ARE ABLE TO HAVE A POSITIVE PRECEPTION, WE CAN SEE THE GOOD IN THINGS, WE ARE SELF-MOTIVATED, AND WE FEEL MORE JOB SATISFACTION.

Q1. Why is a positive perception an important leadership skill?	Q2. What does a positive perception have to do with different personalities and work ethics?	Q3. As a leader, what are some things that you must do in order to have a positive perception?
Answer:	Answer:	Answer:
Why? (Defend Your Answer)	Why? (Defend Your Answer)	Why? (Defend Your Answer)

WHAT ARE SOME OBSTACLES THAT PREVENT YOU FROM HAVING A POSITIVE PERCEPTION?

Case Study 1

Deborah Paz has been the 4th Grade Team Leader for the past eight years. This year, the principal moved her to 3rd Grade Team Leader to help with student achievement and has appointed you to the 4th Grade Team Leader position. Mrs. Paz made it very clear she was not happy with the change and made a few comments towards you in a meeting you didn't appreciate. What next?

Meaningful Teacher Leadership Reflection

Q1. As a Meaningful Teacher Leader, how do you deal with Mrs. Paz's unprofessionalism?

_____

_____

_____

_____

_____

Q2. How do you lead your new team and move forward if she refuses to give you any data or materials?

_____

_____

_____

_____

_____

Q3. What are your three main priorities as you move forward into this new role?

_____

_____

_____

_____

_____

Case Study 2

Sometimes we have students who, over the years, have fallen behind due to behavior issues.

Q1. How can you as a teacher leader help identify these students who have behavior issues vs. true learning issues?

_____

_____

_____

Q2. Who are the people you can utilize?

_____

_____

_____

Q3. How can you share or gather data and distribute it on campus?

_____

_____

_____

MEANINGFUL GOALS

HEALTH

- [ ]
- [ ]
- [ ]
- [ ]
- [ ]
- [ ]
- [ ]
- [ ]

HEART & SPIRITUALITY

- [ ]
- [ ]
- [ ]
- [ ]
- [ ]
- [ ]
- [ ]
- [ ]

FAMILY

- [ ]
- [ ]
- [ ]
- [ ]
- [ ]
- [ ]
- [ ]
- [ ]

COMMUNITY & FRIENDS

- [ ]
- [ ]
- [ ]
- [ ]
- [ ]
- [ ]
- [ ]
- [ ]

MEANINGFUL TEACHER LEADERSHIP CELEBRATIONS

1	
2	
3	
4	
5	
6	
7	

DECISION MAKER

QUESTION: _____

✔ Pro's	✗ Con's
Brain	Heart

SECTION
7

LEADING BY EXAMPLE IS WHEN OUR ACTIONS EMULATE WHAT WE EXPECT FROM OTHERS. LEADING BY EXAMPLE HELPS INSPIRE OTHERS TO WORK AND RESPOND IN WAYS THAT CONTRIBUTE TO ORGANIZATIONAL SUCCESS AND OUTCOMES.

Q1. Why is leading by example an important leadership skill?	Q2. What does leading by example have to do with different personalities and work ethics?	Q3. As a leader, what are some things that you must do in order to lead by example?
Answer:	Answer:	Answer:
Why? (Defend Your Answer)	Why? (Defend Your Answer)	Why? (Defend Your Answer)

WHAT ARE SOME OBSTACLES THAT PREVENT YOU FROM LEADING BY EXAMPLE?

Memorization Icon	"OW" Leadership Reflection	Internalization What does that look like? Draw a picture or symbol.	What do I need to do to nurture this area?
	KNOW: What do I know about leadership?		
	GLOW: What are my leadership qualities that glow? How do I stand out?		
	SHOW: What do I show others? How do others perceive me?		
	GROW: How am I growing as a leader? What am I doing to improve my leadership skills?		
	SNOW: What is cold in my leadership life that requires attention?		
	BOWL: What is in my bowl? What leadership resources do I have?		
	MOW: What is mowing me down and stopping me from moving to the next level of leadership greatness?		

Memorization Icon	"OW" Leadership Reflection	Internalization What does that look like? Draw a picture or symbol.	What do I need to do to nurture this area?
	FLOW: What is flowing smoothly? What are the things going good in the leadership aspect of my life?		
	TOW: What am I towing that may be slowing me down from reaching my full leadership potential?		
	BOW: What am I ready to launch forward?		
	LOW: What is an area of weakness I need to work on?		
	SOW: What am I working on? Remember, you reap what you sow!		
	ROW: What am I rowing towards? Am I going in the right direction?		
	OWE: Who do I owe for mentoring me? What am I taking away from my mentors?		

MEANINGFUL GOALS

HEALTH

☐
☐
☐
☐
☐
☐
☐
☐

HEART & SPIRITUALITY

☐
☐
☐
☐
☐
☐
☐
☐

FAMILY

☐
☐
☐
☐
☐
☐
☐
☐

COMMUNITY & FRIENDS

☐
☐
☐
☐
☐
☐
☐
☐

MEANINGFUL TEACHER LEADERSHIP CELEBRATIONS

1	
2	
3	
4	
5	
6	
7	

PROBLEM SOLVING & PERSEVERING THROUGH OBSTACLES			
OBSTACLE	PLAN A	PLAN B	OUTCOME
OBSTACLE	PLAN A	PLAN B	OUTCOME

SECTION
8

INNOVATION

LEADERS UNDERSTAND THE IMPORTANCE AND VALUE OF INNOVATION. INNOVATION IS PART OF CREATIVITY, PROBLEM-SOLVING, AND ORGANIZATIONAL GROWTH.

Q1. Why is innovation an important leadership skill?	Q2. What does innovation have to do with different personalities and work ethics?	Q3. As a leader, what are some things that you must do to be more innovative?
Answer:	Answer:	Answer:
Why? (Defend Your Answer)	Why? (Defend Your Answer)	Why? (Defend Your Answer)

WHAT ARE SOME OBSTACLES THAT HAVE PREVENTED YOU FROM BEING INNOVATED?

Case Study 1

You are in charge of the math department at your high school. Your campus scores have been consistently good, and slightly above the state average for the last three years. Your principal wants you to take things to the next level. How do you increase student success while leading your department, and maintaining strong professional relationships with your peers? What are your next three steps as a Meaningful Teacher Leader?

Meaningful Teacher Leadership Reflection

Step 1.

_____

_____

Step 2.

_____

_____

Step 3.

_____

_____

Case Study 2

Your school district has a new superintendent. Your principal is now required to make some changes on campus. Your campus is a top school in the region. Your principal's mindset is, "if it isn't broken, don't fix it." Nevertheless, the new superintendent is requesting three changes. The principal asks for your advice. What are your recommendations to the principal and why?

Meaningful Teacher Leadership Reflection

Recommendation 1.

_____

_____

Recommendation 2.

_____

_____

Recommendation 3.

_____

_____

MEANINGFUL GOALS

HEALTH

☐
☐
☐
☐
☐
☐
☐
☐

HEART & SPIRITUALITY

☐
☐
☐
☐
☐
☐
☐
☐

FAMILY

☐
☐
☐
☐
☐
☐
☐
☐

COMMUNITY & FRIENDS

☐
☐
☐
☐
☐
☐
☐
☐

MEANINGFUL TEACHER LEADERSHIP CELEBRATIONS

1	
2	
3	
4	
5	
6	
7	

Problem Solving & Persevering Through Obstacles

Obstacle	Plan A	Plan B	Outcome

Obstacle	Plan A	Plan B	Outcome

Leadership Gallery

Reflect on your Meaningful Teacher Leadership Accomplishments

SECTION
9

PASSION

PASSION COMES FROM HIGH JOB SATISFACTION. WHEN WE LOVE WHAT WE DO, WE GIVE OUR BEST AND ACCOMPLISH GOALS.

Q1. Why is passion an important leadership skill?	Q2. What does passion have to do with different personalities and work ethics?	Q3. As a leader, what are some things that you must do to be more passionate in your career?
Answer:	Answer:	Answer:
Why? (Defend Your Answer)	Why? (Defend Your Answer)	Why? (Defend Your Answer)

WHAT ARE SOME OBSTACLES THAT PREVENT YOU FROM BEING PASSIONATE ABOUT YOUR CAREER AND LIFE?

Memorization Icon	"OW" Leadership Reflection	Internalization: What does that look like? Draw a picture or symbol.	What do I need to do to nurture this area?
	KNOW: What do I know about leadership?		
	GLOW: What are my leadership qualities that glow? How do I stand out?		
	SHOW: What do I show others? How do others perceive me?		
	GROW: How am I growing as a leader? What am I doing to improve my leadership skills?		
	SNOW: What is cold in my leadership life that requires attention?		
	BOWL: What is in my bowl? What leadership resources do I have?		
	MOW: What is mowing me down and stopping me from moving to the next level of leadership greatness?		

Memorization Icon	"OW" Leadership Reflection	Internalization What does that look like? Draw a picture or symbol.	What do I need to do to nurture this area?
	FLOW: What is flowing smoothly? What are the things going good in the leadership aspect of my life?		
	TOW: What am I towing that may be slowing me down from reaching my full leadership potential?		
	BOW: What am I ready to launch forward?		
	LOW: What is an area of weakness I need to work on?		
	SOW: What am I working on? Remember, you reap what you sow!		
	ROW: What am I rowing towards? Am I going in the right direction?		
	OWE: Who do I owe for mentoring me? What am I taking away from my mentors?		

Meaningful Goals

Health

☐

☐

☐

☐

☐

☐

☐

☐

Heart & Spirituality

☐

☐

☐

☐

☐

☐

☐

☐

Family

☐

☐

☐

☐

☐

☐

☐

☐

Community & Friends

☐

☐

☐

☐

☐

☐

☐

☐

MEANINGFUL TEACHER LEADERSHIP CELEBRATIONS

1	
2	
3	
4	
5	
6	
7	

What are five Meaningful Teacher Leadership strengths you have discovered about yourself?

SECTION
10

LEADERSHIP SKILL HIGHLIGHT
OPENNESS

OPENNESS STEMS FROM BEING OPEN TO DIFFERENT VALUES, IDEAS, NEW THOUGHT PROCESSES AND PRECEPTIONS.

Q1. Why is openness an important leadership skill?	Q2. What does openness have to do with different personalities and work ethics?	Q3. As a leader, what can you do to be more open in your career and life?
Answer:	Answer:	Answer:
Why? (Defend Your Answer)	Why? (Defend Your Answer)	Why? (Defend Your Answer)

WHAT ARE SOME OBSTACLES THAT PREVENT YOU FROM BEING OPEN?

Case Study 1

Jennifer Nguyen is completing her master's in Education Leadership in the hope of one day being a principal. Your principal has recommended her to complete the remaining part of her internship hours with you, the Reading Strategist.

Meaningful Teacher Leadership Reflection

What are three key things you wish someone would have told you about leadership that you can share with Jenniffer?

1. _____

_____

2. _____

_____

3. _____

_____

Case Study 2

You were just passed up on a gifted and talented teacher position you have been wanting for the last three years. There is a lot of emotion running through your body. Your principal's rationale was she needs you in the general education classroom to help struggling learners.

Meaningful Teacher Leadership Reflection

1. What is your next move and why?

_____

_____

2. Put yourself in your principal's position. What do you see? And do you agree with her decision?

_____

_____

3. How does being somewhere you're not happy hurt you and you are your student achievement?

_____

_____

MEANINGFUL GOALS

HEALTH

- ☐
- ☐
- ☐
- ☐
- ☐
- ☐
- ☐
- ☐

HEART & SPIRITUALITY

- ☐
- ☐
- ☐
- ☐
- ☐
- ☐
- ☐
- ☐

FAMILY

- ☐
- ☐
- ☐
- ☐
- ☐
- ☐
- ☐
- ☐

COMMUNITY & FRIENDS

- ☐
- ☐
- ☐
- ☐
- ☐
- ☐
- ☐
- ☐

MEANINGFUL TEACHER LEADERSHIP CELEBRATIONS

1	
2	
3	
4	
5	
6	
7	

What are your four core leadership beliefs? Please complete the Leadership Shield.

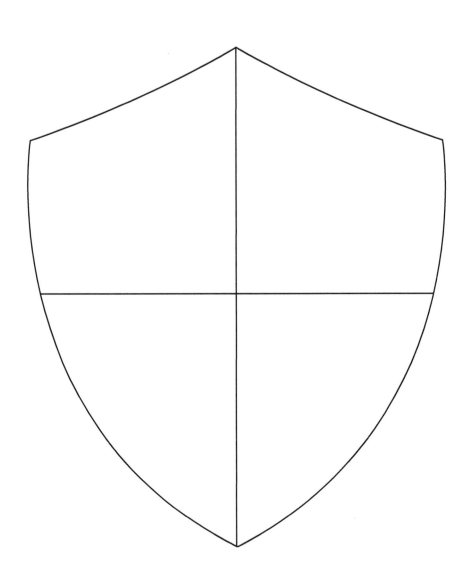

SECTION

II

INSPIRES OTHERS

INSPIRING OTHERS IS THE FOUNDATION FOR LEADERSHIP. ONLY THROUGH INSPIRATION CAN WE WHOLEHEARTEDLY GET TEAM MEMBERS TO FOLLOW US. THROUGH INSPIRING OTHERS, WE PRODUCE GOALS, PURPOSE, AND POSITIVE ENERGY THAT CREATES MOMENTUM.

Q1. Why is inspiring others an important leadership skill?	Q2. What does inspiring others have to do with different personalities and work ethics?	Q3. As a leader, what are some things that you must do to inspire others?
Answer:	Answer:	Answer:
Why? (Defend Your Answer)	Why? (Defend Your Answer)	Why? (Defend Your Answer)

WHAT ARE SOME OBSTACLES THAT PREVENT YOU FROM INSPIRING OTHERS?

Memorization Icon	"OW" Leadership Reflection	Internalization What does that look like? Draw a picture or symbol.	What do I need to do to nurture this area?
	KNOW: What do I know about leadership?		
	GLOW: What are my leadership qualities that glow? How do I stand out?		
	SHOW: What do I show others? How do others perceive me?		
	GROW: How am I growing as a leader? What am I doing to improve my leadership skills?		
	SNOW: What is cold in my leadership life that requires attention?		
	BOWL: What is in my bowl? What leadership resources do I have?		
	MOW: What is mowing me down and stopping me from moving to the next level of leadership greatness?		

Memorization Icon	"OW" Leadership Reflection	Internalization What does that look like? Draw a picture or symbol.	What do I need to do to nurture this area?
	FLOW: What is flowing smoothly? What are the things going good in the leadership aspect of my life?		
	TOW: What am I towing that may be slowing me down from reaching my full leadership potential?		
	BOW: What am I ready to launch forward?		
	LOW: What is an area of weakness I need to work on?		
	SOW: What am I working on? Remember, you reap what you sow!		
	ROW: What am I rowing towards? Am I going in the right direction?		
	OWE: Who do I owe for mentoring me? What am I taking away from my mentors?		

MEANINGFUL GOALS

HEALTH

☐

☐

☐

☐

☐

☐

☐

☐

HEART & SPIRITUALITY

☐

☐

☐

☐

☐

☐

☐

☐

FAMILY

☐

☐

☐

☐

☐

☐

☐

☐

COMMUNITY & FRIENDS

☐

☐

☐

☐

☐

☐

☐

☐

MEANINGFUL TEACHER LEADERSHIP CELEBRATIONS

1	
2	
3	
4	
5	
6	
7	

PROBLEM SOLVING & PERSEVERING THROUGH OBSTACLES

OBSTACLE	PLAN A	PLAN B	OUTCOME

OBSTACLE	PLAN A	PLAN B	OUTCOME

Think about your leadership journey. Where did you start and where do you want to end? Set a leadership goal and note what steps need to be taken to get there.

Start

⇩

⇩

⇩

⇩

Finish

SECTION 12

ACCOUNTABILITY

ACCOUNTABILITY IS THE PROCESS OF BEING RESPONSIBLE FOR THE OUTCOMES OF ACCOMPLISHING GOALS, RESPONSIBILITIES, AND ACTIONS IN WHICH WE ARE COMMITTED TO.

Q1. Why is accountability an important leadership skill?	Q2. What does accountability have to do with different personalities and work ethics?	Q3. As a leader, what are some things that you must do to hold yourself accountable?
Answer:	Answer:	Answer:
Why? (Defend Your Answer)	Why? (Defend Your Answer)	Why? (Defend Your Answer)

WHAT ARE SOME OBSTACLES THAT PREVENT YOU FROM HOLDING YOURSELF ACCOUNTABLE?

Case Study 1

You are the Campus Interventionist. Some of your responsibilities include meeting with teachers to review data and lesson plans. You have been in this position for three months and have found it difficult to complete your tasks because teachers are inconsistent with lesson plans, checking emails, and they're busy with meetings.

Meaningful Teacher Leadership Reflection

1. As a Meaningful Teacher Leader who desires to help everyone increase student achievement, how can you get everyone motivated to take these tasks seriously?

_____

_____

_____

2. What do you need to change for them to change?

_____

_____

_____

3. Why is taking things personally in this situation one of the most toxic things you can do as a Meaningful Teacher Leader?

_____

_____

_____

Case Study 2

The principal wants to work on increasing science scores ten percent above the state average. Please answer the questions below.

Meaningful Teacher Leadership Reflection

1.   What is the first thing the campus leadership team needs to do to get the entire campus to help with this goal?

_____

_____

_____

2. How can leadership activities with students help achieve this goal?

_____

_____

_____

3. How can leadership training for teachers help the campus achieve this goal?

_____

_____

_____

Meaningful Teacher Reflection

Learning looks like

_____

Student achievement is

_____

Meaningful Teacher Reflection looks like

_____

Student reflection increases

_____

Goals are

_____

When I hold myself accountable

_____

_____

MEANINGFUL GOALS

HEALTH

☐
☐
☐
☐
☐
☐
☐
☐

HEART & SPIRITUALITY

☐
☐
☐
☐
☐
☐
☐
☐

FAMILY

☐
☐
☐
☐
☐
☐
☐
☐

COMMUNITY & FRIENDS

☐
☐
☐
☐
☐
☐
☐
☐

MEANINGFUL TEACHER LEADERSHIP CELEBRATIONS

1	
2	
3	
4	
5	
6	
7	

DIGGING DEEPER:
GETTING TO THE ROOT OF THE PROBLEM.

Focus Question 1:

Why?

Focus Question 2:

Why?

Focus Question 3:

Why?

Focus Question 4:

Why?

NOTES

"KNOW"

WHAT DO I KNOW ABOUT LEADERSHIP?

"GLOW"

WHAT IS MY STRENGTH?

HOW DO I STAND OUT?

"SHOW"

WHAT DO I SHOW OTHERS?

HOW DO OTHERS PERCEIVE ME?

"GROW"

HOW AM I GROWING AS A LEADER?
WHAT AM I DOING TO BETTER MY LEADERSHIP SKILLS?

"SNOW"

WHAT IS COLD IN MY LEADERSHIP LIFE AND REQUIRES IMMEDIATE ATTENTION?

"BOW"

What is in my bowl?

What leadership resources do I have?

"FLOW"

WHAT IS FLOWING SMOOTHLY?

WHAT ARE THE GOOD THINGS IN THE LEADERSHIP ASPECTS OF MY LIFE?

"TOW"

WHAT AM I TOWING THAT MAY BE SLOWING ME DOWN FROM REACHING MY FULL LEADERSHIP POTENTIAL?

"BOW"

WHAT AM I READY TO LAUNCH FORWARD?

"LOW"

What is an area of weakness I need to work on?

"SOW"

WHAT AM I WORKING ON?

REMEMBER: YOU REAP WHAT YOU SOW!

"ROW"

WHAT AM I ROWING TOWARD?

AM I GOING IN THE RIGHT DIRECTION?

"OWE"

WHOM DO I OWE FOR MENTORING ME?

WHAT AM I TAKING AWAY FROM MY MENTORS?

"MOW"

WHAT IS MOWING ME DOWN AND STOPPING ME FROM MOVING TO THE NEXT LEVEL OF LEADERSHIP GREATNESS?

About the Author

CHRISTINA DEMARA is the idealistic creator and author of the two leadership doctrines coined as *Meaningful Leadership* and *Early Life Leadership*. She is a Christian, mother, wife, and, educator, public speaker, curriculum creative, and promoter of giving. Her first job, as a high school dropout, was at fifteen, working for the Kirby Vacuum Company. She later completed her bachelor's degree in Interdisciplinary Studies with a minor in Special Education where she found a deep passion for teaching students with exceptionalities. She proudly holds three master's degrees in Special Education, Educational Administration and Leadership, and a third in Curriculum and Instruction from the University of Texas-Rio Grande Valley. She later studied business and leadership extensively through Our Lady of the Lake University in San Antonio, Texas. She has experienced and studied leadership theory, organizational models, and business strategy. She is best known for her creative ideal formulation, and interactive books, *Early Life Leadership Workbook for Girls*, and *I'm Not Broken: The Power of Prayer, Scripture, and Interactive Journaling*. CHRISTINA DEMARA has overcome many obstacles in life through the grace of God and tries every day to motivate others. She enjoys spending time with her family, going to the beach, church, cooking, research, teaching, do-it-yourself projects, and trying new restaurants.

Please connect with Christina! She would love to hear from you!

ChristinaDeMara@gmail.com

ChristinaDeMara.com

EarlyLifeLeadership.com

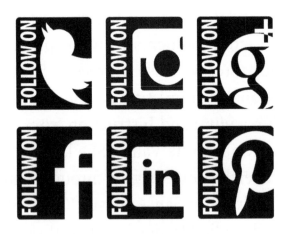

Christina has FREE Facebook groups called:

I Love Reading & Writing

and

I Love Leadership!

You are welcome to join!

Your book reviews help the author and are
extremely appreciated! Please take a few minutes
to leave a review at your place of purchase.

Thank you for your interest
in Christina DeMara's books and resources.

References

"What Is Teacher Leadership?" Instructional Support. Accessed July 14, 2017. http://www.ocmboces.org/tfiles/folder987/whay-whyteacherleadership.pdf.

Boody, Robert M. 1992. "An Examination of the Philosophic Grounding of Teacher Reflection and One Teacher's Experience." Order No. 9231874, Brigham Young University.

Brown, Barrett Chapman. 2012. "Conscious Leadership for Sustainability: How Leaders with a Late-Stage Action Logic Design and Engage in Sustainability Initiatives." Order No. 3498378, Fielding Graduate University.

Carol, Rodgers. "Defining reflection: Another look at John Dewey and reflective thinking." Teachers college record 104, no. 4 (2002): 842-866.

D'Cruz, J., R. (2003). Is the graduate education model inappropriate for leadership development? Healthcare Papers, 4(1), 69-74; discussion 88-90.

DeCristofaro, Ramona. 2016. "A Multi-Case Study Examining Reflection within Collaborative Teacher Inquiry." Order No. 10300212, University of Illinois at Chicago.

Dieker, Lisa DeWitt. 1994. "Using Problem-Solving and Effective Teaching Frameworks to Create Reflective Practitioners." Order No. 9512346, University of Illinois at Urbana-Champaign.

Ellefson, B. A. (1994). Teacher directed professional development (Order No. MM94828). Available from ProQuest Dissertations & Theses Global. (304180244). Retrieved from

Ellefson, Bryan A. 1994. "Teacher Directed Professional Development." Order No. MM94828, University of Lethbridge (Canada).

Giaimo-Ballard, Cindy. 2010. "Key Reflective Teaching Strategies used by Education Faculty in NCATE-Accredited Universities."

Gardner, R. S. (2011). Teacher reflection among professional seminary faculty in the seminaries and institutes department of the church educational system (Order No. 3453587). Available from ProQuest Dissertations & Theses Global. (867818160).

HENRY, CLAIRE. 2016. "A Self Study on how I, as a White, Female Teacher, can use Reflective Strategies to Undergo Critical Reflection." Order No. 10110467, Mills College.

JONES-BRANCH, JULIE. 2009. "Reflective Practice in an Early Childhood Teacher Education Program: A Study of the Components of Learning about and Implementing Reflective Practice." Order No. 3350449, The University of Nebraska - Lincoln.

KERN, BRUCE E. 2010. "Navigating: A Grounded Theory Study of how School Administrators Prepare to Lead." Order No. 3397537, Fielding Graduate University.

LAMM, SHARON LEA. 2000. "The Connection between Action Reflection Learning™ and Transformative Learning: An Awakening of Human Qualities in Leadership." Order No. 9959343, Teachers College, Columbia University.

LINDAMAN, JANE BRANDT. 2005. "Administrative Strategies that Foster Self -Reflective Practice in Iowa Educators as Perceived by Middle -Level Principals and Teachers." Order No. 3166556, University of Northern Iowa.

LoCASALE, DAWN MARIE. 2005. "The Relationship between Novice Teachers' Mentored Guided Reflections and Videotaped Lessons." Order No. 3169658, University of Virginia.

LOVE, DENISE M. 2009. "Thinking on their Feet: Guiding Teacher Candidates to Intuitive Action." Order No. 3379889, Capella University.

MEZIROW, J, (1991). Transformative dimensions of adult learning. The JosseyBass higher and adult education series (1st ed). San Francisco: JosseyBass.

MILLIGAN, R. W. (2014). A transcendental phenomenological study of reflection through exercise (Order No. 3642637). Available from ProQuest Dissertations & Theses Global. (1622150260).

MOWBRAY, BRIDGET KILMER. 2015. "Transformation of Teacher Beliefs regarding Intelligence Theory." Order No. 3704120, Cardinal Stritch University.

PECHAK, C. M. (2007). Structures and processes in international service-learning in physical therapist education: A conceptual model (Order No. 3295489).

PEDRO, JOAN Y. 2001. "Reflection in Teacher Education: Exploring Pre-Service Teachers' Meanings of Reflective Practice." Order No. 3110290, Virginia Polytechnic Institute and State University.

SHEARD, D. J. (2004). Teachers' reflective perceptions on professional learning as influenced by leadership practices (Order No. 3156504). Available from ProQuest Dissertations & Theses Global. (305039468).

STEMME, AMANDA AND SCOTT BURRIS. 2005. "The Art of Teacher Reflection." The Agricultural Education Magazine 77 (6): 25-26.

TAGGART, GERMAINE L. 1996. "Reflective Thinking: A Guide for Training Preservice and In-service Practitioners." Order No. 9637212, Kansas State University.

THOMPSON, J. P. (1998). Principals' perceptions and experiences with mentoring, reflective leadership development, and related variables (Order No. 9901351). Available from ProQuest Dissertations & Theses Global. (304452935).

THE FUTURE OF EDUCATION? (2015). Tech & Learning, 35(11), 12.

TWEEDLE, P. 2002. "The Rationale and Effectiveness of Critical Reflection Strategies for the Continuing Professional Development of Nurses." Order No. U153042, The University of Nottingham (United Kingdom).

WALKER, DEBORAH M. 1997. "A Case Study of Action Research as Staff Development: Facilitating Teacher Reflection." Order No. EP73845, University of Nebraska at Omaha.

WANG, H. X. (2010). A case study of a principal's instructive leadership (Order No. 10441892). Available from ProQuest Dissertations & Theses Global. (1869981996).

WESTHOFF, MAGGIE. 1995. "Mentoring, Concerns, and Job Attitudes of First-Year Teachers." Order No. 9530002, Northern Arizona University.

WILSON, ROBIN BLACK. 2013. "Teacher Interns' Written Reflection in College Assignments." Order No. 3611837, University of Maryland, College Park.